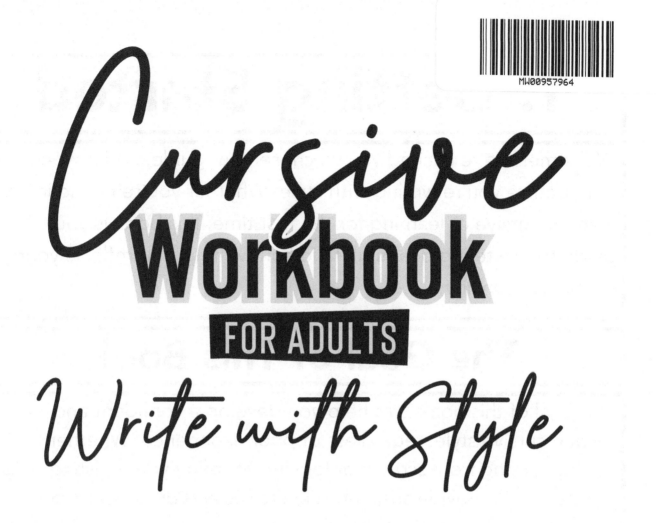

Cursive Workbook for Adults: Write with Style

1: Getting Started

Welcome! We're excited you've chosen our guide, and it won't be long before you're writing with style. Whether you're rekindling a love for cursive or learning for the first time, this book is your guide to mastering beautiful, fluid handwriting that reflects your unique personality.

The Goal of This Book

The goal of this book is to help you develop a confident and unique cursive style, regardless of prior experience. Whether you're starting from scratch or looking to refine your existing skills, this book will provide structured exercises and prompts to get your pencil moving. You'll build a strong foundation through a variety of practice methods, ensuring that each stroke becomes smoother and more natural with time.

By the end of this journey, you will have a personalized cursive style that feels both natural and authentic to you. Whether you're crafting a heartfelt letter, journaling your thoughts, or addressing an envelope, your handwriting will carry a distinct flair that sets it apart.

Consistent practice and dedication are key, and this book is designed to be your guide, supporting you every step of the way. From mastering basic letters to experimenting with personal flourishes, this workbook offers both structure and flexibility, allowing you to grow at your own pace.

The Importance of Handwriting

Handwriting is more than just putting words on paper—it's a deeply personal way to express ourselves. Even in today's digital world, where typing often takes precedence, the act of writing by hand still holds a unique and irreplaceable value. It engages both our mind and body in a way that typing never can. Every stroke of the pen not only captures our thoughts but also reflects the quirks and nuances that make our writing distinctly ours. It's an extension of our personality, a way to make our thoughts feel more tangible.

Cursive writing, in particular, brings an added elegance and individuality to our words. The smooth, flowing strokes of cursive mirror the rhythm of our thoughts, making the act of writing feel more connected and natural. Beyond its beauty, handwriting—whether cursive or print—sharpens our thinking, strengthens our memory, and improves focus. Studies even show that handwriting can enhance cognitive skills, giving us a deeper connection to the ideas we put on the page.

In a fast-paced, digital world, handwriting remains an essential skill. It links us to our past, grounds us in the present, and allows us to express ourselves in a uniquely human way. By taking the time to refine your handwriting, you're not just mastering a skill—you're embracing an art form that's as personal as it is timeless.

Brief History of Cursive Writing

Cursive writing has a rich history, beginning in ancient Rome with Roman cursive, which evolved from Old Roman cursive, used for everyday tasks like letters and business accounts, into New Roman cursive, a more refined form. By the mid-1400s, the demands of commerce led to the development of Secretary Hand, a quick and efficient style that dominated English writing from the 1500s to the early 1700s.

In the 17th century, French Ronde emerged, introduced by Edward Cocker. Initially elaborate, it was later simplified into "fair hand," resembling the cursive we recognize today. The evolution of cursive continued with styles like Cross Writing, popular in the 18th and 19th centuries, where text was written over in a different direction to conserve paper. Copperplate, known for its flowing, slanted letters with thick and thin strokes, became the hallmark of formal writing and calligraphy, showcasing the enduring elegance of cursive through the ages.

In the 19th and early 20th centuries, cursive became an essential part of education with the introduction of the Palmer Method, which emphasized efficiency and legibility, making it the standard for American schools. Later, the Spencerian script added a more decorative flair, influencing penmanship instruction well into the 20th century. Despite the rise of digital communication, cursive has persisted, not only as an elegant way to write but also as a means of personal expression, tying us to centuries of written tradition.

Cursive Throughout History

Roman Cursive

Their way lit by crystals, they continued down the lava gallery which gently sloped, until they came to the intersection of two roads.

Secretary Hand

Bologna Cannes Copenhagen
Florence Grasse Istanbul
Lund Madrid Marseille

French Ronde

Physiognomy Masticate
Sempiternal Harangue
Rubicund Apothegm

Copperplate

Benefits of Developing a Unique Cursive Style

Developing your own unique cursive style allows you to express your individuality through your handwriting. Just as every person's voice is distinct, so too can be their cursive writing. Your cursive style can reflect your personality, creativity, and even your mood, making each piece of writing a true representation of who you are. Take a look at the personal style of a few well known people.

pour pleurer pour vous mes pauvres enfants; adieu, adieu! Marie Antoinette **Marie Antoinette**

Good luck with everything! Bill Gates **Bill Gates**

credeva che lui fosse cagione che non ebbe la permissione di ballarin teatro. addio. non scordarvi di me io sono sempre il vostro fedele fratello amadeo Wolfgango Mozart **Mozart**

cuando desperté y dije: ¡Zócalo! ya es rete tarde para irme a la escuela'. (20 de Agosto de 1929.) te adora tu Frida. **Frida Kahlo**

Benefits of Developing a Unique Cursive Style

Improves Writing Speed and Efficiency

One of the key advantages of cursive writing is its efficiency. The connected, flowing letters allow for quicker writing compared to print, where each letter is separate. This can be particularly beneficial for note-taking, journaling, or any situation where writing speed is important. As you develop your unique style, you will find that your writing becomes smoother and more fluid, allowing you to capture your thoughts effortlessly.

Adds a Personal Touch to Written Communication

In an increasingly digital world, handwritten notes and letters have become a rare and cherished form of communication. A beautifully written cursive note can convey warmth, sincerity, and personal attention in a way that typed text cannot. Whether it's a thank-you note, a birthday card, or a personal letter, your unique cursive style adds a special touch that makes your communication stand out and feel more meaningful.

Handwritten Vs. Typed Note

Dearest Grandma,
Thank you for flying out to attend my graduation party. It meant the world to have you there to celebrate this milestone with me.
With Love,
Martha Jo

Dearest Grandma,
Thank you for flying out to attend my graduation party. It meant the world to have you there to celebrate this milestone with me.
With Love,
Martha Jo

Making Cursive Your Own

Personal Style Over Rigid Textbook Formats

Cursive writing is not about rigidly adhering to a specific set of rules or formats. It's about finding a style that feels natural and authentic to you. While learning the basics is essential, the true beauty of cursive writing lies in its flexibility and the ability to make it uniquely yours. Instead of focusing on perfect textbook letter forms, think of cursive writing as an art form where your individuality can shine.

Experimentation with Different Letter Forms

Experimentation is key to developing your own style. Try out different ways of forming letters and see what feels most comfortable and aesthetically pleasing to you. Don't be afraid to mix and match styles or to modify traditional forms. For example, you might prefer a more looping style for your 'g' or a more angular approach to your 'r.' The goal is to find a balance between readability and personal flair.

Tips for Developing a Consistent Personal Style

1. Analyzing Your Current Handwriting: Begin by examining your current handwriting. Identify the characteristics that you like and want to keep. Pay attention to aspects such as the slant of your letters, the loops, and the spacing between words.

2. Identifying Elements You Like and Want to Keep: Make a list of the elements in your handwriting that you enjoy. This could be anything from the way you form certain letters to the overall flow of your writing. Keeping these elements will help ensure that your new style feels familiar and comfortable.

3. Gradually Incorporating Changes and Improvements: Start incorporating new elements slowly. Practice writing a few letters or words with your new style each day. Gradual change will help you adapt without feeling overwhelmed. Over time, these small adjustments will lead to a significant transformation in your handwriting.

4. Practice Sheets for Experimenting with Different Styles: Use the provided practice sheets to experiment with various styles. Try writing the same sentence in different ways, adjusting the slant, size, and spacing of your letters. This practice will help you discover what feels right for you.

FAQ's Before Getting Started

What if my writing looks messy?

Messiness is a common concern. Focus on one aspect of your writing at a time, such as the consistency of your letter sizes or the smoothness of your connections. With regular practice, your writing will become more refined.

How do I maintain consistency?

Consistency comes with practice. Set aside a few minutes each day to write in cursive. Repetition will help reinforce your new style and make it second nature. Additionally, pay attention to the rhythm of your writing, ensuring that each letter flows smoothly into the next.

What if I'm not creative?

You don't need to be creative to write in cursive or develop your own style! Begin with the basics and gradually experiment with new elements shown in this guide!

2: Letters

Aa Bb Cc Dd
Ee Ff Gg Hh
Ii Jj Kk Ll
Mm Nn Oo Pp
Qq Rr Ss Tt
Uu Vv Ww Xx
Yy Zz

Uppercase Letters

Uppercase letters in cursive are often more elaborate than lowercase, and can add a touch of flair to your writing. These letters typically serve as the starting point of a sentence or a proper noun, making them an important part of your cursive style. While learning the traditional forms, please experiment with variations, and see what feels natural to you. Remember, uppercase letters are larger and often more intricate, so take your time mastering each one.

Below, you'll find a variety of examples for each letter, showcasing different styles and interpretations to serve as inspiration for developing your own version of each letter. Use the space below the examples to practice writing each letter multiple different ways. Don't be afraid to get creative and even artistic with your uppercase letters!

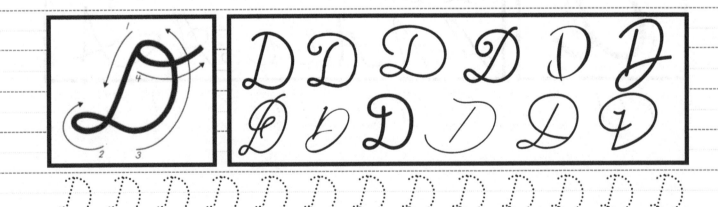

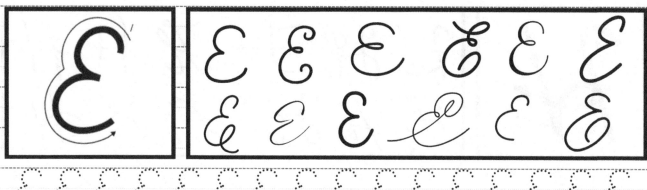

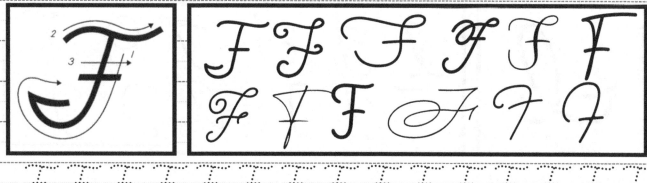

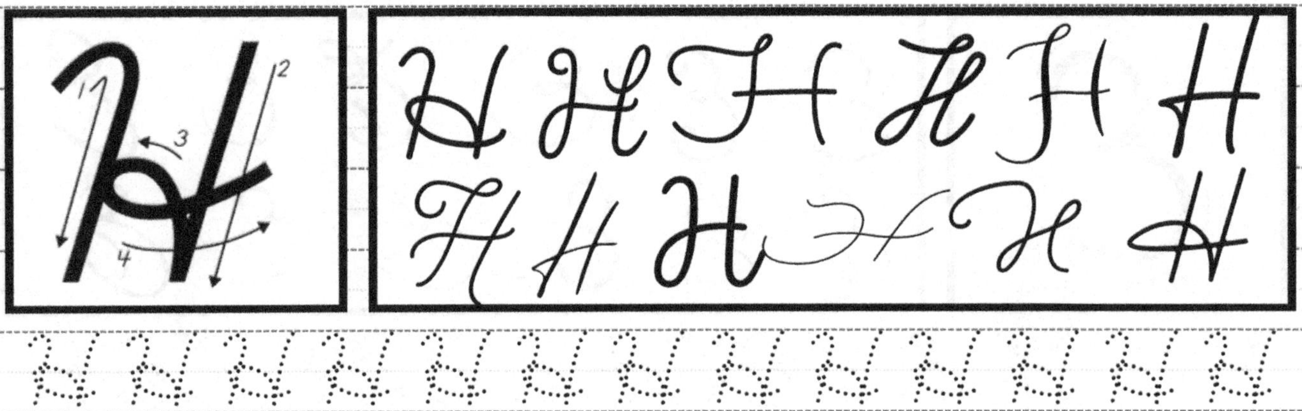

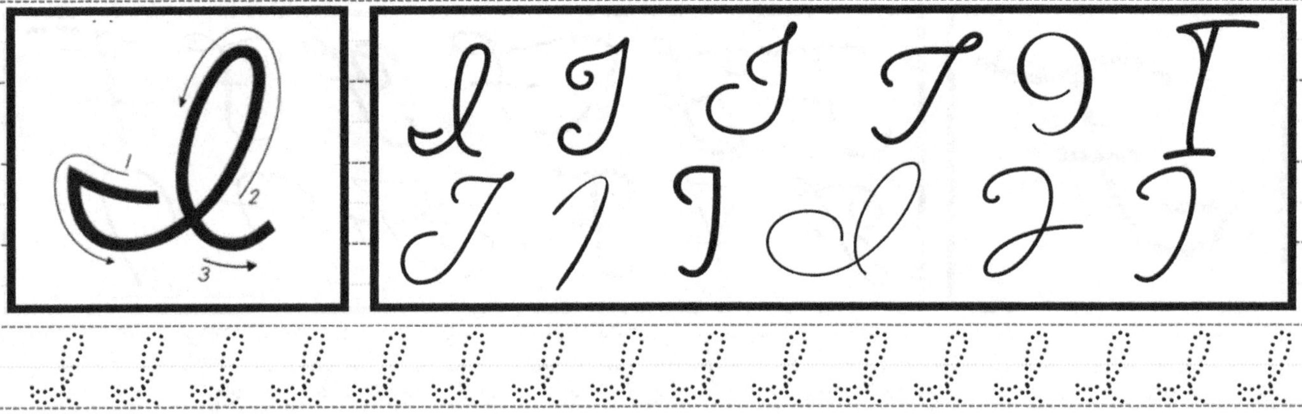

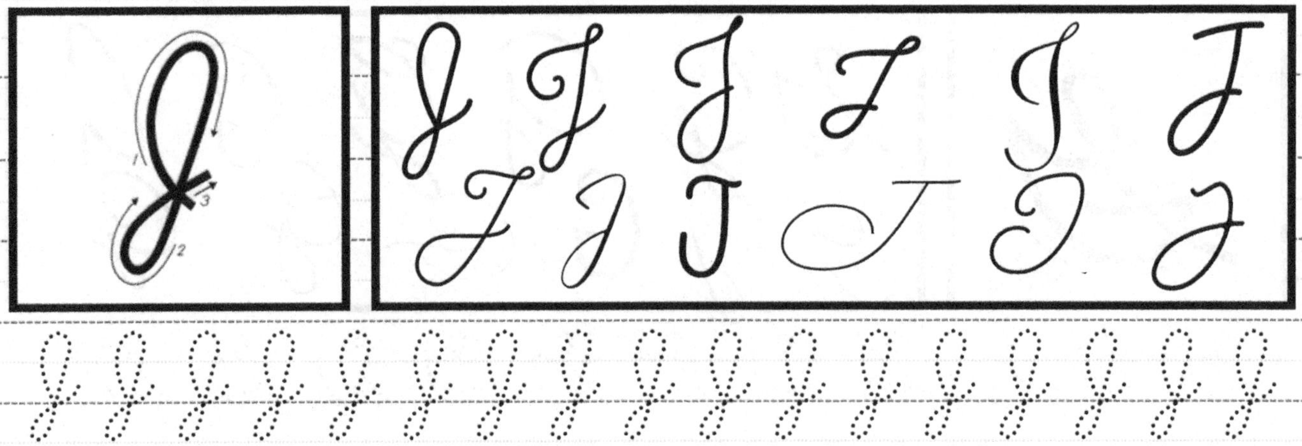

K K K K K K K K

K K K K K K K

KKKKKKKKKKKKKKKKKKKK

L L L L L L L

L L L L L L L

LLLLLLLLLLLLLLLLLLLL

M M M M M M M

M M M M M M M

m m m m m m m m m m m

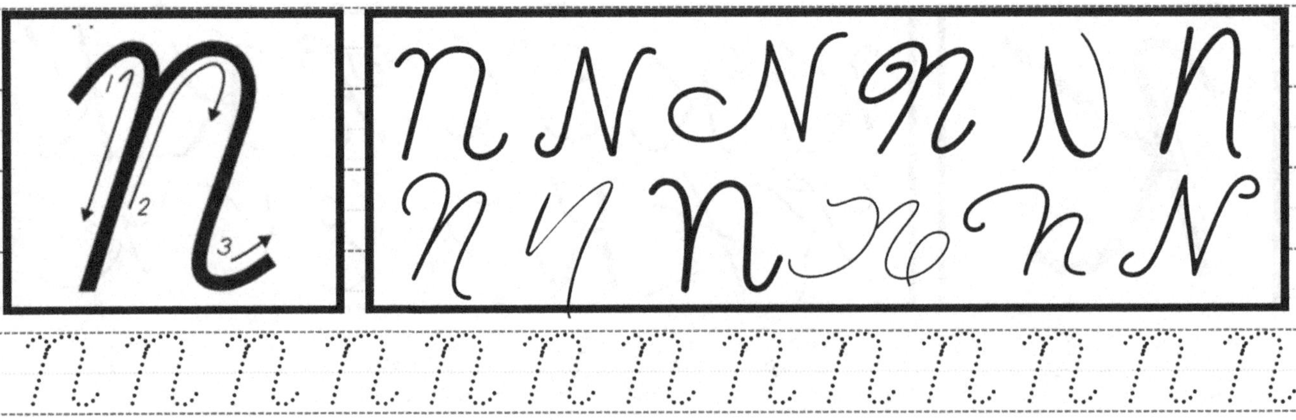

n N N N N N
n n n n n n
nnnnnnnnnnnnnn

O O O O O O O
O O O O O O
OOOOOOOOOOOOO

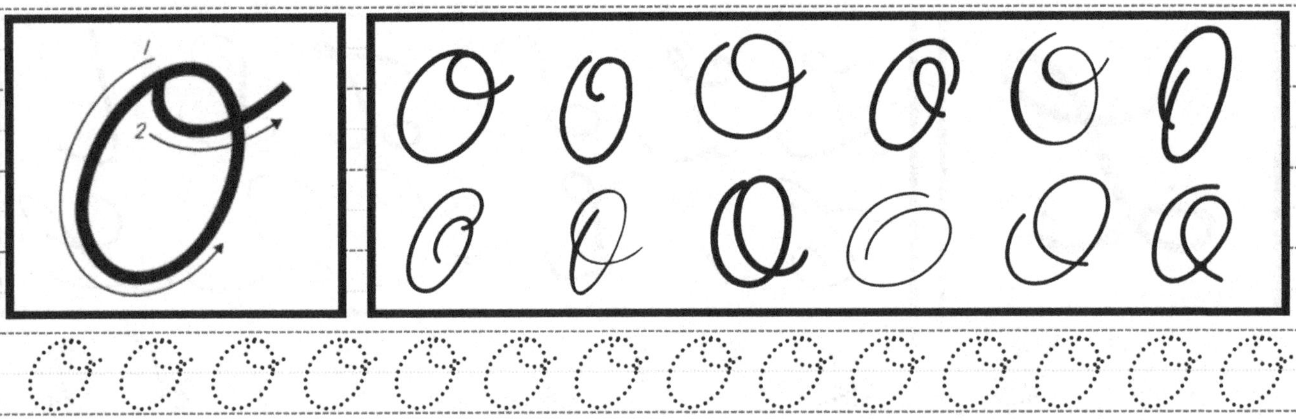

P P P P P P P
P P P P P P
PPPPPPPPPPPPPP

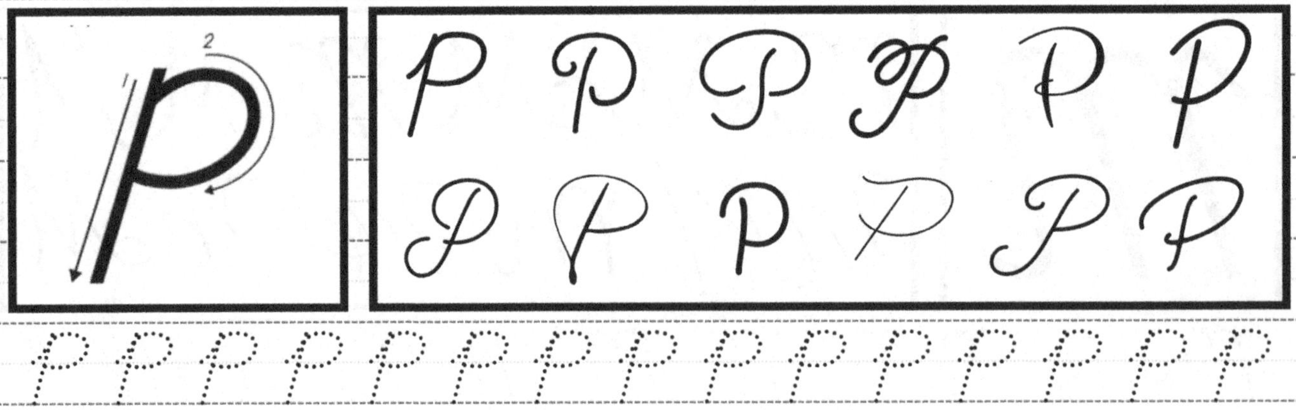

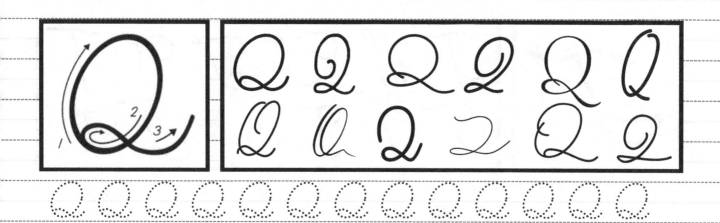

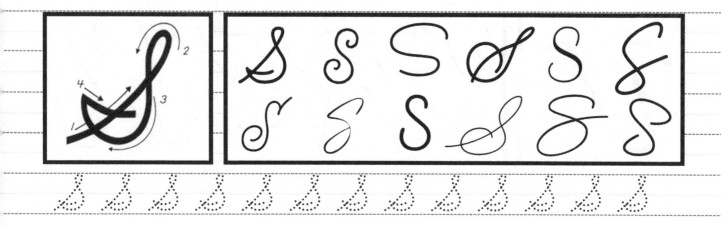

T T T T T T T T
T T T T T T

U U U U U U U
U U U U U U U

V V V V V V V V
V V V V V V V V

W

W W W W W W
W W W W W W

w w w w w w w w w w w w

X

X X X X X X
X X X X X X

X X X X X X X X X X X X

Y

Y Y Y Y Y Y
Y Y Y Y Y Y

y y y y y y y y y y y y y y

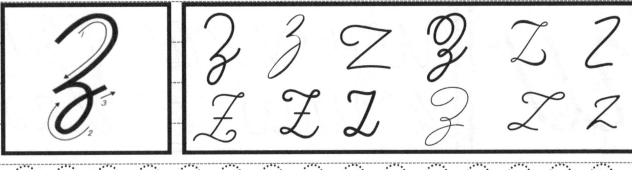

Lowercase Letters

Lowercase letters in cursive are the backbone of your writing, creating the smooth, connected flow that defines cursive script. These letters are generally smaller and simpler than their uppercase counterparts, designed to connect seamlessly with one another. As you practice, focus on the consistency of size and slant, as these are key to achieving a cohesive and fluid handwriting style. Don't be afraid to adapt the strokes slightly to suit your natural hand movement.

Below, you'll find a variety of examples for each letter, showcasing different styles and interpretations to serve as inspiration for developing your own version of each letter. Use the space below the examples to practice writing each letter multiple different ways.

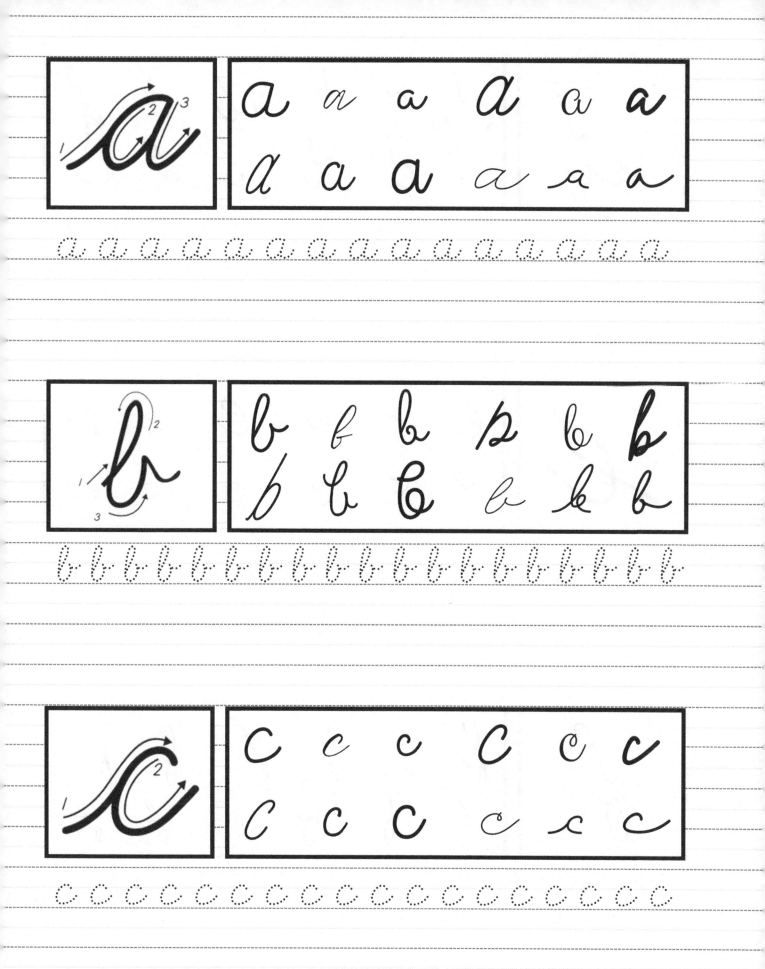

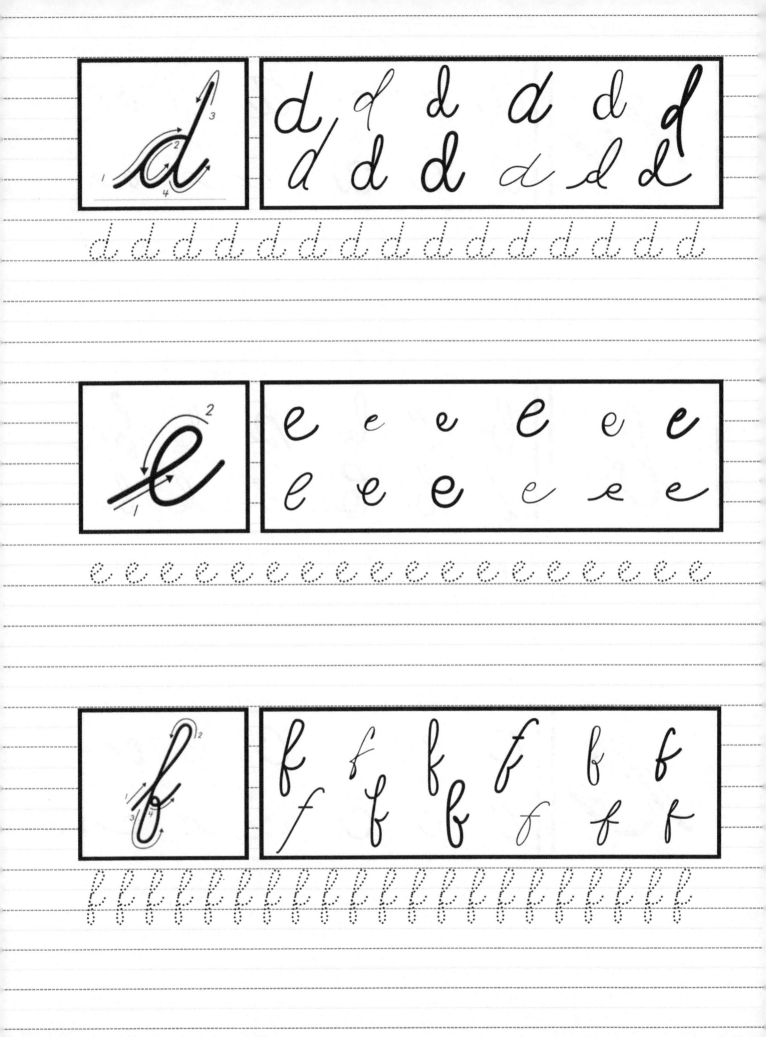

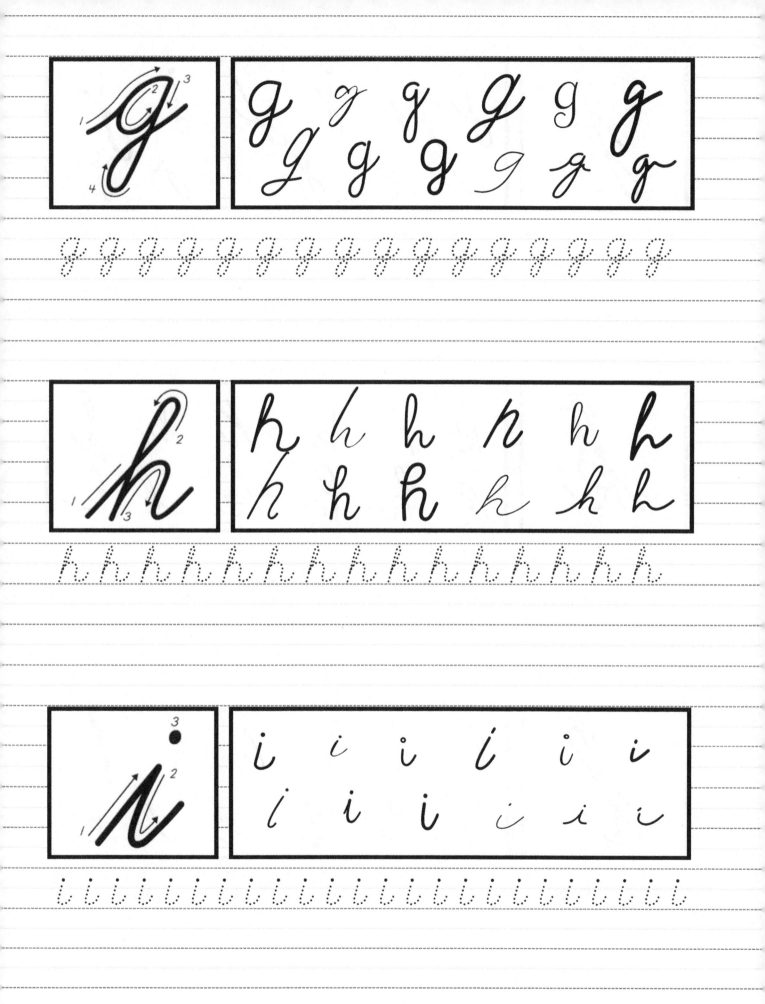

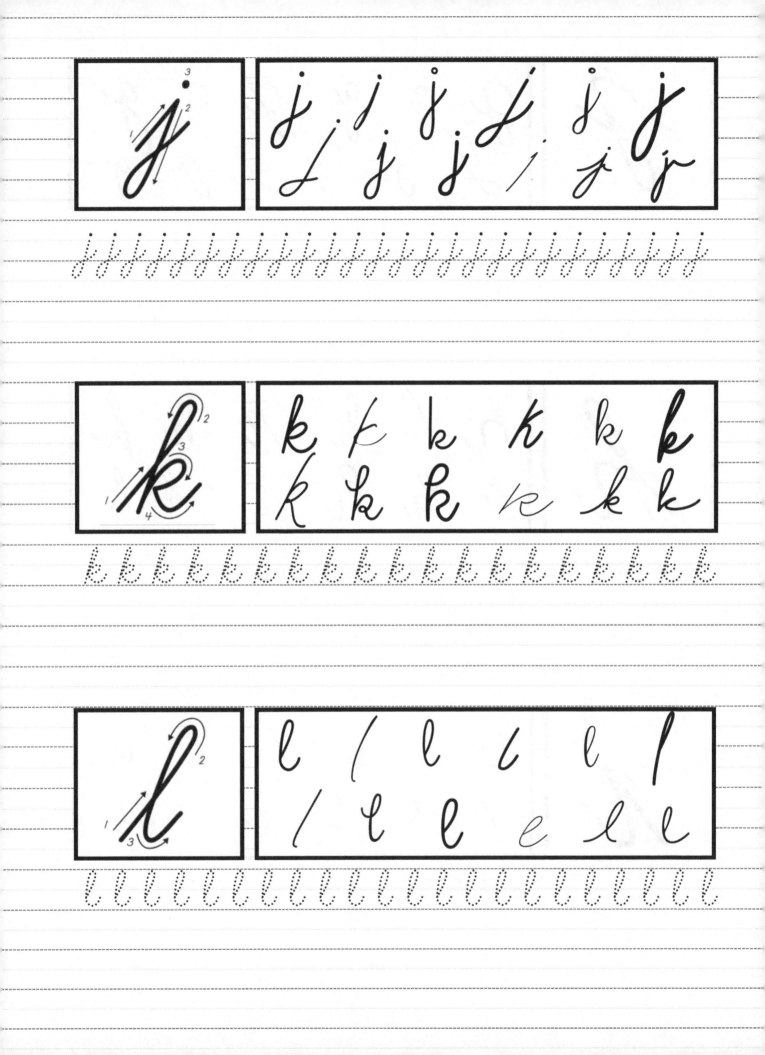

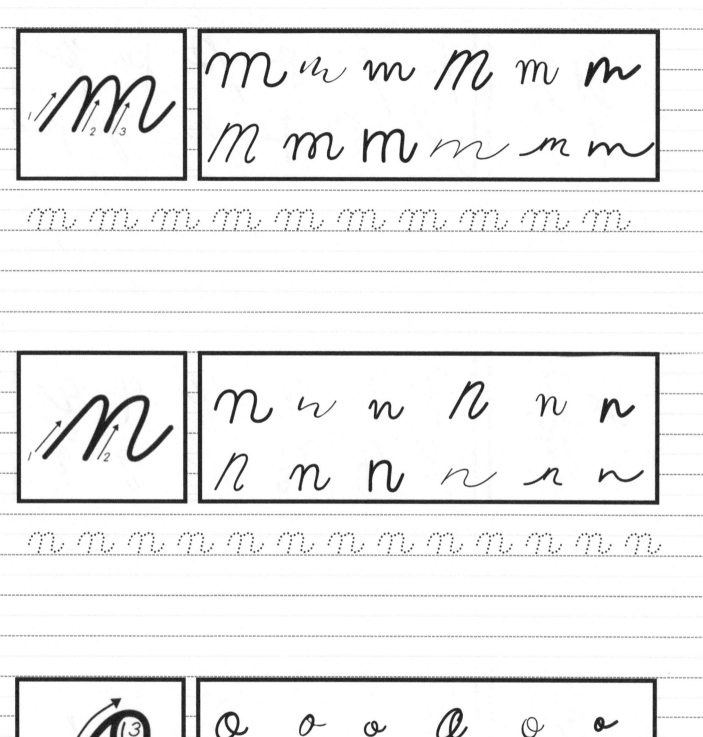

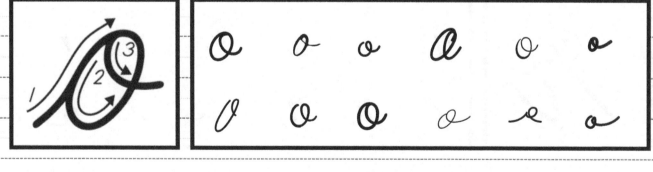

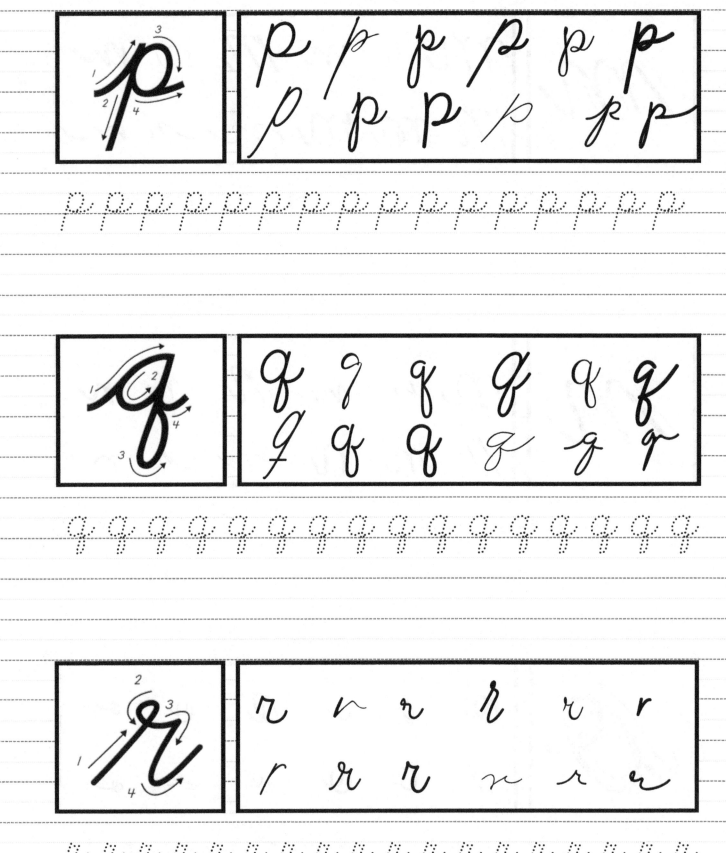

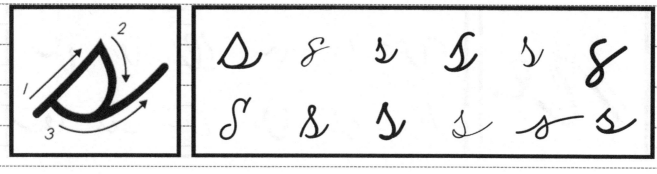

ᗪ ᗪ

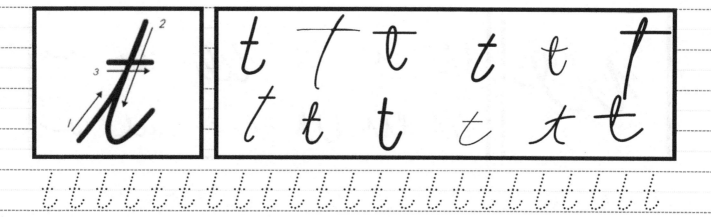

t t t t t t t t t t t t t t t t t t t t t t

ᴜ ᴜ

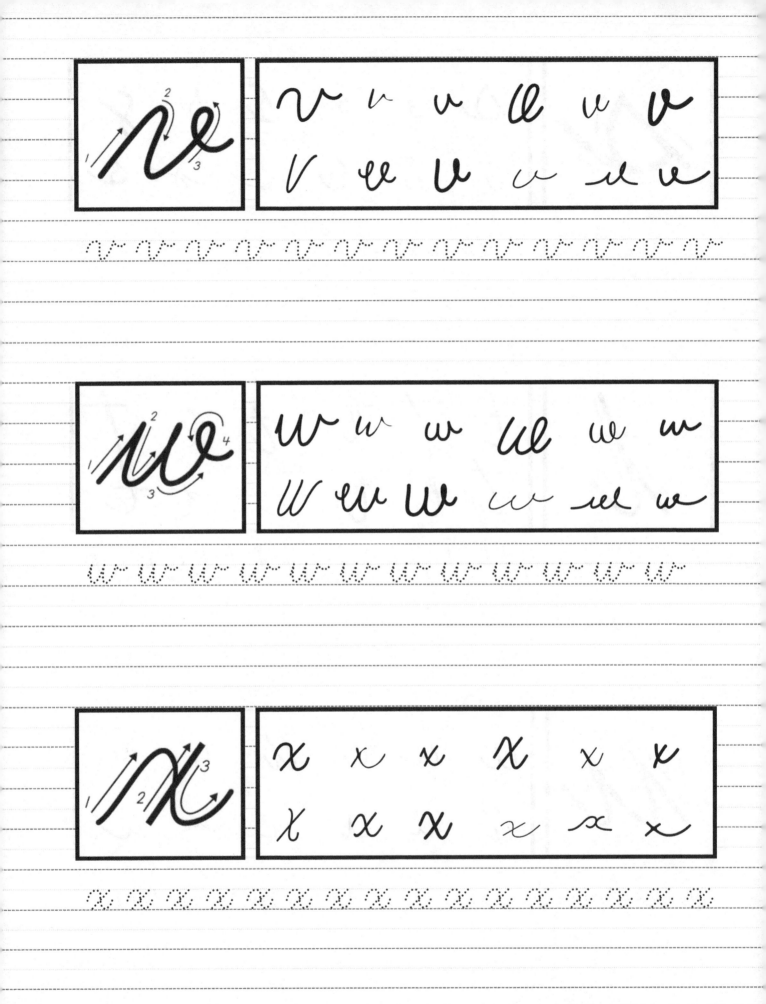

Connecting Letters

Mastering the connection of letters is what truly brings cursive writing to life. The fluid, continuous motion from one letter to the next is what gives cursive its distinctive elegance and efficiency. When connecting letters, it's important to maintain a consistent slant, size, and spacing to ensure that your writing flows smoothly and remains legible. Pay attention to how the ending stroke of one letter leads naturally into the beginning stroke of the next. This seamless transition is key to achieving a unified and cohesive script.

As you practice connecting letters, you'll notice that certain combinations may feel more natural than others. It's perfectly normal to encounter some pairs or triplets that require a bit more attention. Focus on maintaining an even pressure on the pen, as this will help create smooth connections and prevent any abrupt or jagged transitions.

Examples in multiple styles are shared below. Use the practice space to work on connecting letters in your own style. Mix in connections between upper and lowercase, with a variety of letters.

Au At Af ar ap an at au ab

An Ab af ad al an aur ap

Ba Br Ba be bo bu bl by bs

Ba Br Be bu bl ba by bi br

Ch Cl Ca cr cu ce ci cy ck

Ch Cl Ca cr ce cs ck cy ci

Du Dr De do da de ds dy dd

Du Dr De di dd dy do ds

Ev Ep Ea eq er es en em ex

Ev Ep Em ea ef ex eg eq

Fr Fa Fe fu fo fy fi ft ff

Fr Fa Fe ff ft fi fo fr fr fu

Ga Gr Go gl gn gs gi gh gg

Ga Gh Gn gl gg gs ge gi

He Ha Hi hs hu ht ho he hl

He Ha Hi ho ht hs hr hl

In Id It iu ix if ic im ig

In Id If im is in ic ig im

Ju Jo Je ja jo ji jy jo jr

Ju Jo Je ju ja jy ji jo je jr

Ke Kn Ki ke kl ks ki ka ck

Ke Kn Ko kl ky ks ka ke

Lo Le La lw lp ly lm lb ll

Lo Le Lu ll ls lk ly la lc

Ma My Mo me mp mm ms my

Ma My Me mi mm mp

No Na Nu nc nn ng nc nz nd

No Na Ni nn nd nk nt ni

Or On Od ov of op ox ow oz

Or On Ov ot os ox ov oz

Pl Po Pi pr pa pu pe ps py

Pl Po Pe pp pl pr py pt pi

Qu Qe Qa qu eq aq iq sq qu

Qu Qe Qa qu sq eq iq aq

Re Ri Ra rs rt rb rl rp rf

Re Ri Ra rn rt rp rk rd rs

St So Sm su ske sm sy ss sq

St So Sm si st sur sp sm

Th Ti To ta th ts tl tt Ty

Th To Tn ta tur tu te ts ti

Un Ur Ul up uv ut um ul uv

Un Up Ul ud uv ub um

Ve Va Vo vy ve vw va vi vs
Ve Va Vo vi vy vw vu

Wr We Wo wa wn wl wc wk
Wr We Wi wf wt wl wk

Xa Xe Xo ex ax ix xe xl xy
Xa Xe Xo xl xi ex ax xy

Yo Ya Ye yi ye ya ly py dy
Yo Ya Ye yp ya dy fy by

Ze za Zo za ze zi zz iz oz

Ze za Zo zz zy zl za iz

Letters FAQ's

Why do my letters look uneven?

Uneven letters often result from inconsistent pressure or spacing. Focus on applying consistent pressure as you write, ensuring that each stroke is smooth and even. Additionally, pay close attention to the spacing between letters and words, as uneven spacing can disrupt the overall flow of your writing.

How can I improve my letter connections?

Focus on the transition between each letter, ensuring that the ending stroke of one letter naturally flows into the beginning stroke of the next. Pay attention to maintaining consistent pressure and spacing as you connect letters, as this will help create a more fluid and cohesive script.

I'm struggling with certain letters!

If you're struggling with certain letters, it's important to break them down into their basic strokes. Start by practicing the individual components of the letter slowly and deliberately until you feel more comfortable with the motions.

Letters FAQ's

Why do my letters lean too much to one side?

Letters that lean too much, either to the left or right, are often the result of inconsistent slant or hand positioning. To correct this, try tilting your paper slightly to find a more comfortable angle, and practice writing with a consistent slant guide. Focusing on keeping your wrist steady and your strokes even can help you achieve a more balanced and uniform slant.

How can I make my letters more uniform in size?

Achieving uniform letter size requires consistent attention to the height and width of each letter. Using lined or grid paper can help guide you in maintaining even proportions. Practice writing slowly and focus on keeping each letter within the same height and baseline. Regular practice will help you develop muscle memory for consistent letter sizing.

Why does my writing feel cramped?

Cramped writing often results from writing too fast or gripping the pen too tightly. Try loosening your grip and slowing down your pace to give your hand more freedom to move. Also, ensure you're leaving adequate space between words and letters to make your writing feel more open and relaxed. Using lined paper can help guide your spacing and improve the flow of your handwriting.

Congratulations on completing the letters section!

You've built a solid foundation by mastering each letter, both individually and through connections. Now that you're confident with the basics, it's time to take the next step and start forming words, where your handwriting will truly come to life.

3: Words

Combining letters into words is where your cursive writing really starts to come together. This is the stage where you'll begin to see the true fluidity of cursive, as each letter seamlessly connects to the next, creating a smooth, continuous line of writing. The key to forming beautiful, readable words is maintaining consistent spacing between each letter and ensuring fluid connections that carry the rhythm of your writing. As you progress, you'll notice how the smoothness of your transitions makes your handwriting appear more polished and professional.

One important aspect of writing words in cursive is learning to trust the flow of your pen. Rather than focusing on each individual letter, try to think of the word as a whole, guiding your pen with a steady rhythm from start to finish. This will help your words look cohesive and balanced, and prevent choppy or disjointed connections. As you practice, feel free to experiment with different speeds to find what works best for you, always remembering that consistent motion is the key to creating fluid, legible words.

In the practice space provided, you'll find a variety of words written in different cursive styles to inspire you as you develop your own. These examples are meant to spark creativity and show how cursive can take on many different forms. Additionally, we've included traceable words for you to practice letter connections and consistency. Below these examples, you'll have extra practice space where you can write words in your own style or focus on the areas you feel need more attention. Use this space to experiment and refine your words until they feel completely natural.

Apple   answer   ask   apple

Amazing   ant   arms   arrow

Amelia   artist   and   autumn

Brad   bright   blue   begin

Benjamin   bad   busy   balance

Bravely   break   big   blossom

Calmly   cat   city   caring

Chris   curious   cool   catch

Cedric   complete   cry   clean

Daisy   dog   delight   direct

David   dimple   dance   dare

Daddy   down   develop   done

Elegant   eat   enjoy   event

Emily   elevate   early   explore

Everyone   echo   eager   effort

Frank   fun   fair   future

Fiona   fearless   flower   full

Flower   friends   feels   forward

Grace   goal   glow   garden

Georgia   great   genuine   give

Grandma   gal   gift   guess

Hero   hope   happy   humble

Hannah   hug   help   house

Home   healthy   habit   humor

Imagine   iced   inspire   idea

Isaac   impact   interest   invest

Ivy   integrity   instinct   igloo

Journey   joy   jump   joke

Julia   journal   job   juggle

January   join   jewel   joyful

King   key   keep   known

Kevin   kite   knock   kick

Knoxville   kiss   knack   kitten

Lovely   light   laugh   loud

Luke   learn   legacy   leave

Liam   laxitive   listen   letter

Mother magic moon mixer

Mia memory move moment

Matthew match mount mine

Noble nice narrow nurture

Natalie navigate new nest

November never now neat

Oscar open original eats

Olivia often observe orbit

Ocean offer olden outside

Panther peace pink plan

Peter passion plant park

Paige proud place party

Queen quiet quest quick

Quench quality quaint quote

Quinton quiz quench quite

Ranger rise respect reflect

Ryan relax run resilient

Rachel ready nest rainbow

Sarah strength smile shine

Saturday small spirit smart

Sammy start safe special

Thomas trust teach talent

Taylor thrive take touch

Thursday today try team

Useful uplift unit under

Ulrich umpire urge ultra

Uber upbeat useful upper

Value   value   vision   view

Vivian   voice   view   visit

Voyage   vanish   vital   vent

Willy   wise   wish   went

Wendy   worthy   witty   warm

Welcome   win   world   wait

Xerox   exit   xenial   axe

Xavier   extra   expect   excel

Xenon   xylophone   explore   axe

Yay   yes   youth   yearn

Young   yellow   yard   yesterday

Yolanda   yet   you   yummy

Zebra   zest   zone   zeem

Zane   zigzag   zip   zero

Zombie   zeal   zillion   zesty

4: Sentences

Now that you've gained confidence in writing individual letters and words, it's time to combine all your skills and start practicing full sentences. In this chapter, we'll guide you through important aspects of sentence formation, broken down into manageable sections. Each section will focus on a specific aspect of writing cursive sentences, such as letter size, spacing, slant, and punctuation. You'll have the opportunity to practice and refine each element individually, followed by longer practice sentences to bring it all together.

Take your time with each section, practicing the provided sentences first by tracing and then by writing in your own style. Remember, consistency is key, and the more you practice, the more natural and fluid your handwriting will become.

Consistent Letter Size and Spacing

Maintaining consistent letter size and spacing is crucial for both readability and the overall look of your writing. Focus on keeping your letters the same height, and make sure the space between your words is even. Consistency here creates a cohesive, balanced appearance.

Instructions: Trace the sentences and then write them on your own with a focus on consistent letter size and spacing.

Consistency is key with cursive writing.

Try to keep all letters the same height.

Maintain the same space between each letter in each word.

A little progress each day adds up.

Practice makes perfect!

Consistency leads to improvement.

Writing by hand is a joy.

Consistent Spacing Between Words

Not only must you maintain consistent spacing between letters within each word, you must also maintain consistent spacing between each word in the sentence. Whether your words are close together, medium spaced, or widely spaced, they should maintain a uniform look.

Instructions: Experiment with different spacing between words within the sentence. Try writing them with the words close together, medium-spaced, and further apart. See what feels natural and what looks the best to you.

Write this sentence with the words close together.

Now write this with the words medium spaced.

Finally, write this sentence with wide spaces between words.

Maintaining a Consistent Slant

A uniform slant gives your cursive writing a clean, polished look. Whether you prefer a slight slant or a steeper angle, focus on keeping the slant consistent across all your letters and words. A steady wrist and consistent paper positioning will help you achieve this.

Instructions: Experiment with different slants. Try writing sentences with no slant, a slight slant, and an extreme slant. See which angle looks best to you!

Write this with minimal slant.

Write this with a little bit of slant.

Write this with a lot of slant!

This sentence is written with the slant that I think looks best.

Balancing Speed and Control

Balancing speed with control is important for maintaining legibility without sacrificing flow. Start by writing slowly to ensure accuracy, then gradually increase your speed while maintaining control over your letters and connections. Eventually, you'll be able to write quickly and beautifully.

Instructions: Experiment with different speeds. Try writing sentences with slow, medium, and fast. This is the time to make mistakes and test your limits!

Start by writing this slowly.

Now pick up the speed a little bit.

Write this sentence quickly but comfortably.

Finally, write this as fast as you can!

Faster, faster! How fast can you write?

Which speed felt the most comfortable?

I am writing this sentence at the pace that feels comfortable and accurate.

I know how to balance speed and accuracy for beautiful writing.

Punctuation and Capitalization

Proper use of punctuation and consistent capitalization enhances the clarity and readability of your writing. A common trick in cursive writing is to write the sentence first and add punctuation afterward to maintain a smooth flow. After finishing the sentence, go back to carefully place punctuation marks.

Instructions: Write the sentences, ensuring proper punctuation. It is up to you whether you punctuate as you write each word, or go back to add punctuation after completing the entire sentence.

"Believe in yourself," she said.

Our Monday plans: Visit New York City, ride the "Night Train", and see a Broadway show.

It's incredible—you've improved so much in just a few weeks!

My trip to Italy (which I've been planning for years) is finally happening next month!

Wait... are we really going to the concert on Friday, or did I mishear?

"Great job on the project," exclaimed Sarah, "but don't forget the deadline is tomorrow!"

More Practice Sentences

Don't watch the clock; do what it does. Keep going.

Success is not final, failure is not fatal: it is the courage to continue that counts. —Winston Churchill

Happiness is not by chance, but by choice.

You miss 100% of the shots you don't take. —Wayne Gretzky

A day without laughter is a day
wasted.

You are never too old to set
another goal or dream a new
dream. —C.S. Lewis

Success usually comes to those
who are too busy to be looking for
it.

It always seems impossible until
it's done.

Be yourself; everyone else is
already taken.

Keep your face always toward
the sunshine, and shadows will
fall behind you.

Dreams don't work unless you
do.

Difficult roads often lead to
beautiful destinations.

The journey of a thousand miles
begins with a single step.

I am a master of writing
cursive sentences.

5: Developing Your Style

Now that you've laid the foundation with the basics of cursive writing, it's time to take it a step further and infuse your handwriting with your own personal touch. Cursive is more than just a skill—it's an art form that reflects your unique personality and style.

Whether your style is subtle or extravagant, you'll discover a range of techniques that transform your cursive into something truly special. As you work through these personal touches, you'll find that your handwriting begins to take on a life of its own, becoming a true extension of who you are.

In developing your personal style, the key is to experiment and find what feels most natural and authentic to you. Don't be afraid to try out different techniques—whether it's adding a playful loop to your descenders, experimenting with varying slants, or incorporating elegant flourishes to your capital letters. The more you practice and adjust, the more your unique style will emerge. Remember, there's no "right" way to do it; your style should be a reflection of your creativity and individuality.

As you continue, embrace the imperfections and quirks that make your handwriting distinctly yours. Cursive is meant to flow, not to be rigid or forced. Over time, these small variations will evolve into signature elements of your writing, something that's instantly recognizable as yours. So take your time, enjoy the process, and watch your cursive transform into an art form that is unmistakably you.

Slant and Size Adjustments

Slightly varying the slant or size of your letters can create a dynamic and visually interesting look. By adjusting the slant or alternating the size of certain letters, you can emphasize specific words or letters, adding depth and character to your writing.

size smaller, slant tilt

Practice writing the following words, and any other words you'd like, while varying the slant or size of your letters. Notice how these adjustments affect the overall appearance and feel of your writing.

Slanted   Slanted   Slanted

smaller   smaller   smaller

bigger   bigger   bigger

tilted   tilted   tilted

Loops on Ascenders and Descenders

Loops on ascenders and descenders add a decorative flair to your writing, giving it an elegant and unique touch. By extending the tops of ascenders like 'l' and 'h' with loops, or elongating the tails of descenders like 'g', 'y', and 'j', you can create a flowing and sophisticated style that stands out.

highly   loop   jog

Write the following words, focusing on adding decorative loops to the ascenders and descenders. Experiment with different loop sizes to see what feels most natural to you.

Happy   Happy   happy

Loopy   loopy   loop

Grace   grace   golden

Elegant   joy   laugh

Flourished Capitals

Flourished capital letters add a sense of importance and style to your writing, perfect for starting sentences or emphasizing key words. By adding extra curves or lines to capitals like 'A', 'B', 'H', and 'K', you can give your handwriting a bold and artistic flair that draws attention.

Hugs and Kisses   Dr. Berry

Write the following words, starting each one with a flourished capital letter. Try adding extra curves or lines to make your capitals stand out.

Flourish   Victory   United

Kevin   Prayer   Ready

Grace   Never   Mother

Amelia   Queen   Crisp

Underlines and Swashes

Underlines and swashes are perfect for adding emphasis or a stylish finish to your writing. Underlining important words or names can highlight their significance, while adding swashes at the end of words creates a graceful and connected appearance.

I miss you very much.

Tiffany Berry

Write the following words, adding underlines beneath them or swashes at the end. Use these elements to add emphasis and flair.

Your Son   Go!   I miss you

Just wait till your father gets home!

I love you more than you know.

Tail Extensions

Tail extensions involve lengthening the tails of certain letters, such as 'r' or 's', to connect seamlessly with the next letter or word. This technique creates a sense of fluidity and continuity in your writing, making your script appear more connected and dynamic.

Stargazing   stargazing

Practice writing the following words, focusing on extending the tails of 'r' and 's' into the next letter or word. Aim for smooth, fluid connections.

Whisper   Howdy   Wild Child

adventures   Hey   dream

I love stargazing in the summer.

You're invited to the party!

Double Strokes

Adding a second line to the downstrokes or upstrokes of letters like 't', 'd', 'k', 'j', and 'y' can give your writing a bold and eye-catching appearance. This technique can create a shadow effect or make your letters appear more prominent, adding depth and dimension to your script.

tada   joy   kid

Write the following words, adding a second line to the downstrokes or upstrokes of letters. Experiment with the thickness and placement of these double strokes.

Today   Kind   Hello

joyful   angry   alarmed

flick   jumpy   tada

flower   hushed   smiles

Dotted and Dashed Lines

Dotted and dashed lines along the downstrokes of letters can add a whimsical and playful touch to your writing. This technique is perfect for adding a bit of flair to letters like 'i', 'j', and 'f', making your script feel more lively and creative.

joy   fish

Write the following words, adding dots or dashes along the downstrokes of letters like 'i', 'j', and 'f'. Try different patterns to add a whimsical touch.

Imagine   Joy   Fun

fish   inspire   lovely

faith   astounded   dreams

Unique Letter Endings

Finishing your letters with curls, spirals, or flicks can give your writing a unique and personalized touch. This technique works particularly well with letters like 'r', 's', and 'z', allowing you to add a bit of character and style to your script.

lover   kiss   jazz

Practice writing the following words, focusing on adding curls, spirals, or flicks to the endings of the last letter of the word. Experiment with different styles to see what fits your personal style.

Lover   Kiss   Jazz

crazy   sweet   swean

mashed   curls   hug

stop   bunch   star

Heart or Star Accents

Replacing the dots on 'i' and 'j' with small hearts or stars adds a playful and charming element to your writing. This technique can be used sparingly to add a touch of whimsy and personal flair, making your script more fun and unique.

whimsical   joy

Write the following words, replacing the dots on 'i' and 'j' with small hearts or stars. Use these accents sparingly to add a playful touch.

Whimsical   joy   jump

Sincerely   joyful   invite

justice   juggle   icing

Darling   Kisses   admire

Exaggerated Curves

Adding exaggerated curves to the middle of letters like 'e', 'm', and 'n', or at the end of descenders like 'y', 'g', or 'j' can create a more fluid and connected appearance. This technique brings a graceful, flowing elegance to your writing, making each word feel more continuous and sophisticated. The exaggerated curves help add a dramatic flair, making your script stand out with style.

money

Write the following words, incorporating exaggerated curves into the middle strokes of letters like 'e', 'm', and 'n', or to descenders like 'y', 'g', or 'j'. Play with different levels of curvature to enhance both fluidity and expressiveness.

Memory   Journey   Harry

elegant   stammer   flowing

timeless   bloom   laugh

Crossbar Variations

Experimenting with the crossbars on letters like 't' and 'f' allows you to add a variety of styles to your writing. Whether you make them wavy, double-lined, or extended, crossbar variations can add flair and individuality to your script.

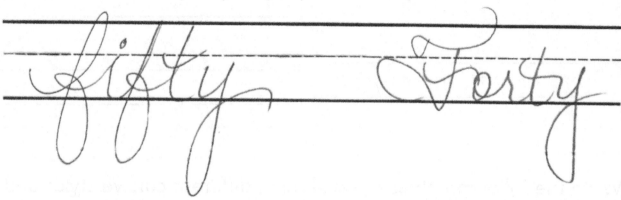

Write the following words, focusing on the crossbars of letters like 't' and 'f'. Experiment with different styles, such as wavy or extended crossbars, to see what adds flair to your writing.

Flutter   *Faith*   *Toys*

thoughtful   *fantasy*   *trust*

Festival   *gift*   *artist*

Perfect   *outfit*   *soft*

Combination of Styles

Mixing traditional cursive elements with modern or artistic styles can lead to a unique and personalized script. By incorporating calligraphy techniques or blending different cursive styles, you can create a handwriting style that is truly your own.

Dearest Mother,

Sincerely,

Allison

Write the following phrases, combining different cursive styles and techniques. Experiment with mixing traditional and modern elements to create a style that is uniquely yours.

Always stay curious and creative.

Embrace your personal style.

Find joy in the little things.

Your handwriting tells your story.

More Practice

Write the following phrases, adding personal touches of your choice. Repeat this exercise with different flourishes, experimenting to find personal touches that you like. Try to work towards finding personal touches that feel natural to you, and practice them until they become a natural part of your writing.

I love you

Good morning

Take care

I miss you

Best wishes

Congratulations

Thank you

Good luck

See you soon

Well done

Happy Birthday

Be well

Have a great day

Your Friend

With deepest sympathy

More Practice

Stay true to yourself.

Dream big, shine bright.

Love deeply, laugh often.

Create your own destiny.

Kindness is always in style.

Courage begins with a single step.

Joy is found in simplicity.

6: Practical Applications

By now, you've developed a solid foundation in cursive writing, from mastering individual letters and words to crafting full sentences with your unique style and personal flair. You've taken the time to explore and refine your handwriting, making it a true reflection of your personality. Now, it's time to bring those skills into the real world.

This chapter is all about putting your cursive to use in everyday situations. Whether it's jotting down a grocery list, writing a heartfelt letter, or creating a beautifully handwritten invitation, cursive can add a touch of elegance and personality to your daily tasks. We'll explore various scenarios where cursive writing can be both practical and enjoyable, helping you see how you can incorporate your newfound skills into your everyday life. From personal notes to professional communication, there are countless opportunities to let your handwriting shine.

As you work through this chapter, think about the personal impact that handwritten cursive can have in a world dominated by digital communication. The act of writing by hand can make your messages feel more thoughtful and personal, whether you're crafting a thank-you note or adding a special touch to your daily planner. Cursive isn't just a tool for formal occasions—it's a skill that can be woven into the fabric of your everyday life, helping you communicate with elegance, care, and a personal touch. Let's dive into some practical applications and start making cursive a part of your daily routine.

Journaling

Journaling is a wonderful way to express your thoughts, reflect on your day, and record your memories. Writing in cursive adds a personal and intimate touch to your journal entries, making them feel more meaningful. Use this opportunity to let your thoughts flow freely while practicing your cursive style.

Practice writing short journal entries based on the prompts given.

Today, I felt

A goal I have this year is

Note Taking

Whether you're in a meeting, attending a lecture, or simply jotting down ideas, taking notes in cursive can help you write more quickly and efficiently. The flowing nature of cursive allows you to capture your thoughts without lifting your pen as often, making it easier to keep up with fast-paced information.

Scribble down some notes about what you've learned in this cursive workbook so far. Write quickly but clearly, as if you're in a fast paced note taking scenario.

Keys to Clear Letters:
- *consistent slant*
- *smooth pace*
- *fluid connections*
- *letter size*

Developing Personal Style:

List Making

From grocery lists to to-do lists, writing lists in cursive can make even the most mundane tasks feel more organized and satisfying. Cursive allows you to write quickly while still keeping your lists neat and easy to read. Plus, it adds a touch of elegance to your everyday tasks.

Create a grocery list or a to-do list for your day. Focus on keeping your handwriting clear and consistent while writing quickly.

Grocery List: Grocery List:
apples
bacon

eggs
salad
peanut butter

To Do: To Do:
call Mom
mow the lawn
laundry
study for test

Handwritten Letters

Writing a letter to a friend or family member in cursive is a personal and heartfelt way to stay in touch. The flow and elegance of cursive can make your words feel more sincere and thoughtful. Whether it's a thank you note or a simple hello, your handwriting adds a personal touch that digital communication lacks.

Write a short letter to a friend, focusing on expressing your thoughts clearly and warmly. Pay attention to the consistency of your slant and spacing as you write.

Dear
It feels like ages since we last caught up, and I've been thinking about you lately. How are you?

Invitations

Handwritten invitations are a beautiful way to invite someone to a special event. Using cursive for your invitations adds a touch of class and warmth that printed invitations can't replicate. Whether it's for a birthday, a dinner party, or a casual get-together, your handwritten invitation will stand out.

Write a sample invitation for an event. Focus on making your writing elegant and easy to read, with flourished capitals and smooth connections.

Please join us for Alex's graduation party! We're celebrating this special milestone with good food, great music, and plenty of fun.

You are cordially invited to

Addressing Envelopes

Addressing envelopes in cursive not only looks beautiful but also gives your correspondence a professional and polished appearance. The smooth, flowing lines of cursive can make even the smallest detail, like an address, look special.

Practice writing addresses like you're addressing an envelope. Make sure to keep your writing clear and legible, with a focus on consistent letter size and spacing.

Mr. John Doe
123 Main Street
Anytown, CA 54321

Brett & Maria Watson
99 South Cedar Street
Unit 71
Tampa, FL 30510

Place Cards for Events

Handwriting place cards in cursive adds an elegant touch to any event, whether it's a wedding, a dinner party, or a formal gathering. The personal touch of cursive writing helps guests feel welcomed and appreciated.

Write out place cards for a fictional event, focusing on making your cursive clean and decorative.

Table 1:
Emma Johnson
William Davis
Ruby Rose
Zoe Rodriguez

Table 2:

Daily Planner Entries

Using cursive in your diary or planner helps make daily planning more enjoyable. It can also make your entries look more organized and elegant, turning a simple task into something you look forward to.

Fill out a sample page for a daily planner, focusing on neatness and consistency.

Day: Monday

8:00am: *Breakfast with mom*

10:00am: *Zoom call for with boss*

12:00pm: *Yoga with Joe*

2:00pm: *Study for Friday's test*

4:00pm:

6:00pm:

Day: Tuesday

8:00am:

10:00am:

12:00pm:

2:00pm:

4:00pm:

6:00pm:

Recipe Cards

Writing your favorite recipes in cursive on recipe cards can add a personal and nostalgic touch to your kitchen. It also makes sharing recipes with friends and family more special.

Write out your favorite recipe on a recipe card. Focus on clarity and adding any personal touches to make the card uniquely yours.

Chocolate Chip Cookies:
3 cups flour
Half cup sugar
Half cup brown sugar
3 lbs. chocolate chips
2 lbs butter

Chicken Noodle Soup:

Thank You Cards

A handwritten thank you card in cursive is a simple yet powerful way to show your appreciation. The effort you put into writing by hand can make your gratitude feel even more genuine and heartfelt.

Write a thank you card to someone who has helped or supported you recently. Focus on making your message clear and warm, with elegant flourishes.

Dear

Thank you for being a part of our special day! Your presence at our wedding meant the world to us, and we're so grateful you could celebrate this milestone with us.

Dear

Guest Books

Signing a guest book in cursive adds a touch of elegance and personal connection. Whether it's at a wedding, an event, or even at home, your entry in cursive will stand out and be remembered.

Write a message in a guest book as if you were attending a special event. Focus on making your writing neat and memorable.

Congratulations on your big day! We had a blast celebrating with you.
With Love,

Scrapbooking

Adding handwritten captions or notes to your scrapbook in cursive can make your memories even more special. Cursive writing adds a personal and artistic touch to your photos and keepsakes.

Write captions or short notes for a scrapbook page, focusing on making your handwriting decorative and fitting for the theme.

Summer Vacation 2024

Sweet Caroline, 2 years old

Amy's 50th Birthday Party!

Writing Quotes

Handwriting your favorite quotes in cursive can be a meditative and inspiring practice. The elegance of cursive writing can make the words resonate even more, turning them into a piece of art.

Write out a favorite quote in cursive, focusing on the flow and beauty of your handwriting. Add personal touches like flourishes or underlines to make it your own.

"I hated every minute of training, but I said, 'Don't quit. Suffer now and live the rest of your life as a champion.'" — Muhammad Ali

"Champions keep playing until they get it right." — Billie Jean King

Signatures

Developing a unique and stylish signature in cursive is a great way to leave your mark. Your signature is often seen as a reflection of your personality, so making it distinctive can be a rewarding practice.

Practice writing your signature in different styles, experimenting with flourishes, loops, and underlines to make it uniquely yours.

John Smith   *John Smith*

John Smith   *John Smith*

John Smith   *John Smith*

7: Writing Prompts

In this chapter, you'll find a series of writing prompts designed to help you further refine your cursive skills while expressing your thoughts and creativity. These prompts are meant to inspire you, challenge you, and encourage you to put your cursive writing into practice. As you work through each prompt, focus on maintaining the fluidity and consistency of your handwriting, while also allowing your personal style to shine through.

As we near the end of your cursive practice journey, this is your chance to truly put all that you've learned into action. These prompts are not just about perfecting your handwriting—they're about using your cursive as a tool for expression. The journey doesn't end here, but these exercises will give you the confidence to take your cursive into the real world, where you can use it in everyday writing.

There's no right or wrong way to approach these prompts—let your imagination guide your pen, and enjoy the process of bringing your words to life on the page. Use this chapter as an opportunity to not only practice your cursive but also to explore new ideas, reflect on your experiences, and express yourself in a way that feels authentic and true to you. This is your moment to make your cursive truly yours.

Overcoming Challenges

What is one challenge you had to overcome in your cursive journey? Describe how you overcame it and what you learned from the experience.

Describe Your Cursive Style

Write a paragraph describing the unique characteristics of your cursive writing style. What do you like most about it?

Cursive in Daily Life

When do you plan to use cursive in your real life? Write about the occasions and tasks where you see yourself using cursive.

Favorite Cursive Letters

Which cursive letters do you enjoy writing the most and why?
Write a few sentences incorporating those letters.

Improvement Goals

What aspects of your cursive writing would you like to improve? Write about your goals and the steps you plan to take to achieve them.

Gratitude List

Write a list of things you are grateful for and explain why each one is meaningful to you.

Favorite Memories

Describe one of your favorite childhood memories in detail. What made it so special?

Life Lessons

Write about a valuable life lesson you have learned. How has it influenced your actions and decisions?

Future Aspirations

What are your dreams and aspirations for the future? Describe the steps you plan to take to achieve them.

Choose Your Superpower

If you could have any superpower, what would it be and why? How would you use it in your daily life?

Dinner with a Historical Figure

If you could have dinner with any historical figure, who would it be and why? What questions would you ask them?

A Day in Your Dream Job

Describe what a typical day would be like if you had your dream job. What tasks would you enjoy the most?

Favorite Book Character

Who is your favorite character from a book, and why do you relate to them? Write about a scenario where you interact with this character.

Funny Childhood Story

Write about a funny or embarrassing moment from your childhood. What happened, and why is it a memorable story?

Book Review

Write a review of this book, "Cursive Workbook for Adults: Write with Style". Be honest and detail the things you did and didn't like about the book.

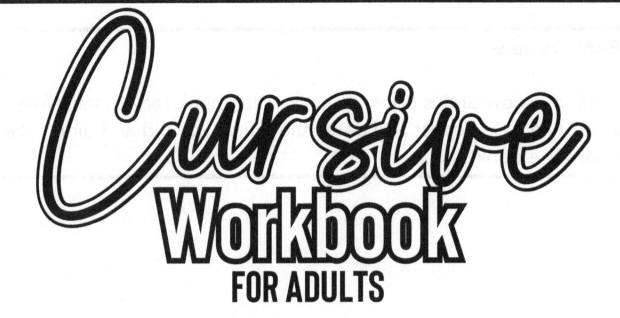

If you enjoyed this book

We'd Love Your Feedback

BRAINWAVE BOOKS

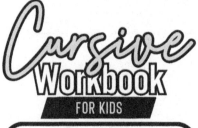

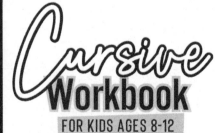

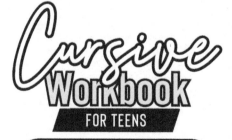

Coming Soon!

Practice Pages

Made in the USA
Monee, IL
01 December 2024

71885286R00070